AuB

W9-BZB-998

First Facts™

Positively Pets

Caring for Your Fish

by Adele Richardson

Consultant:
Jennifer Zablotny, DVM
Member, American Veterinary Medical Association

Capstone
press®

Mankato, Minnesota

First Facts is published by Capstone Press,
151 Good Counsel Drive, P.O. Box 669, Mankato, Minnesota 56002.
www.capstonepress.com

Library of Congress Cataloging-in-Publication Data
Richardson, Adele, 1966–
    Caring for your fish / Adele Richardson.
    p. cm. —(First facts. Positively pets)
    Summary: "Describes caring for a fish, including supplies needed, feeding, cleaning,
health, safety, and aging"—Provided by publisher.
    Includes bibliographical references and index.
    ISBN-13: 978-0-7368-6386-5 (hardcover)
    ISBN-10: 0-7368-6386-9 (hardcover)
    1. Aquarium fishes—Juvenile literature 2. Aquariums—Juvenile literature. I. Title.
II. Series.
SF457.25.R53 2007
639.34—dc22   2005035854

Editorial Credits
Becky Viaene, editor; Bobbi J. Wyss, designer; Kim Brown, illustrator; Kelly Garvin,
    photo researcher/photo editor

Photo Credits
Ardea/Jean Michel Labat, 19; Capstone Press/Karon Dubke, 5, 6, 7, 8–9, 10–11, 12, 13;
Comstock Images, cover; Corbis/Aaron Horowitz, 16–17; Dwight R. Kuhn, 15;
Minden Pictures/Wil Meinderts/Foto Natura, 20; Shutterstock/ijansempoi, 21

Capstone Press thanks Pet Expo, Mankato, Minnesota, for their assistance with this book.

1 2 3 4 5 6 11 10 09 08 07 06

Table of Contents

So You Want to Own Fish?

Colorful fish dart through the water. You want fish from the pet store. But are you ready for the responsibility?

Learn how to care for fish before you get some. Good care will help keep your fish healthy.

Cold-water fish, like me, are easier to care for. I don't need a water heater in my tank like my warm-water friends. Wait until you're an experienced owner to get a warm-water fish, like an angelfish.

Supplies and Setup

Before bringing fish home, you have setting up to do. Fill an **aquarium** with water and gravel. Check the water temperature with a special **thermometer**.

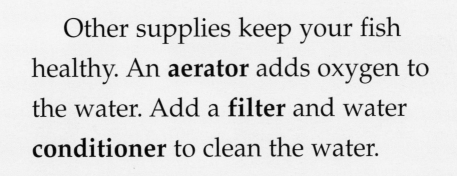

Other supplies keep your fish
healthy. An **aerator** adds oxygen to
the water. Add a **filter** and water
conditioner to clean the water.

Into the Tank

After two days, the aquarium is ready for a few fish. Float the fish bags in the aquarium.

After about 20 minutes, your fish are used to the water. Use a net to scoop them out of the bags and into the water. After about five weeks, the tank is ready for more fish.

feeding Your Fish

You can buy fish food at a pet store. Fish eat in the morning and at night.

Your job is to make sure they don't eat too much. Give your fish enough food to eat for about five minutes. That's about a pinch.

Cleaning

Cleaning the aquarium helps your fish stay healthy. About every two weeks you'll need to scrub the aquarium. But don't use soap or your fish will get very sick.

Use a **siphon** to clean the gravel and remove water. Clean until the water level drops a few inches. Then, add a few inches of fresh water and conditioner.

Signs Your Fish Are Sick

Sometimes fish get sick. They may move slowly or look droopy. Check for white spots or torn fins. Fish usually won't eat when they are sick.

If one of your fish is sick, call a **veterinarian** or pet store. They can likely tell you how to help your sick fish.

Not all veterinarians treat fish. Find a vet for me before I get sick.

mouth fungus

15

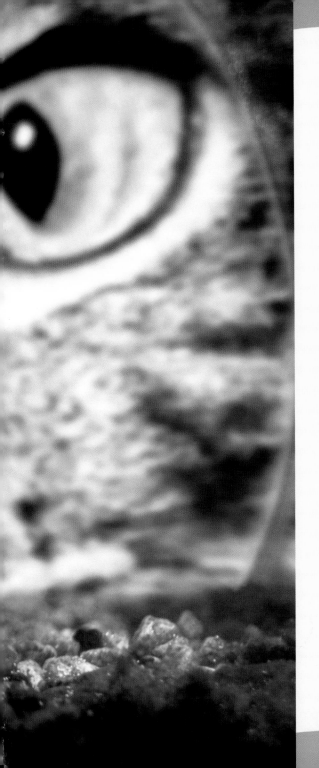

Fish Safety

Good fish owners keep other pets away from the aquarium. An aquarium cover stops a curious cat from hurting your fish. It also stops your fish from jumping out.

Sudden loud noises scare me. So please don't let anyone tap on the tank!

Your Fish's Lives

Many fish never stop growing. They can live for 2 to 20 years. Make sure the tank is big enough so your fish have room to exercise. With good care, your fish will remain healthy and active their entire lives.

You've probably seen goldfish digging up gravel in an aquarium. That's because goldfish are bottom-feeders. Wild goldfish and their relatives, called carp, dig up sand at the bottom of lakes. Just like your goldfish, they're looking for food.

Decode Your Fish's Behavior

- Fish swim on their sides when they're sick. Sick fish also rub against the tank and breathe quickly.

- Fish hide when they are scared or uncomfortable. Fish with many places to hide often hide less because they feel safe.

- Are your fish sleeping? Sleeping fish usually stay in one place. But fish don't have eyelids, so their eyes are always open. Even while sleeping, most fish move their fins.

Glossary

aerator (AIR-ray-tor)—a machine that supplies water with oxygen

aquarium (uh-KWAIR-ee-uhm)—a glass tank where pets, including hamsters, hermit crabs, and fish, are kept

conditioner (kuhn-DISH-uh-nur)—a product that removes unsafe chemicals, like chlorine, from aquarium water

filter (FIL-tur)—a device that cleans liquids or gases as they pass through it

siphon (SYE-fuhn)—a bent tube through which liquid can drain upward

thermometer (thur-MOM-uh-tur)—an instrument that measures temperature

veterinarian (vet-ur-uh-NER-ee-uhn)—a doctor who treats sick or injured animals; veterinarians also help animals stay healthy.

Read More

Blackaby, Susan. *Fish for You: Caring for Your Fish.* Pet Care. Minneapolis: Picture Window Books, 2003.

Hibbert, Clare. *Fish.* Looking After Your Pet. North Mankato, Minn.: Smart Apple Media, 2005.

Loves, June. *Fish.* Pets. Philadelphia: Chelsea Clubhouse, 2004.

Internet Sites

FactHound offers a safe, fun way to find Internet sites related to this book. All of the sites on FactHound have been researched by our staff.

Here's how:

1. Visit *www.facthound.com*

2. Choose your grade level.

3. Type in this book ID **0736863869** for age-appropriate sites. You may also browse subjects by clicking on letters, or by clicking on pictures and words.

4. Click on the **Fetch It** button.

FactHound will fetch the best sites for you!

Index